Cracking the $500 Billion Federal Market:

The Small Business Guide to Federal Sales

Richard White

Cover design: Thomas Luparello

ISBN Number: 978-0-6152-0067-5

This book was printed in the United States of America.

Foreword

The following is a sequel to my first book, <u>Rolling the Dice in DC: How the Federal Sales Game is Really Played</u>. Unlike <u>Rolling the Dice</u>, this latest work is written specifically with the small business owner in mind. It touches upon many of the themes of the first book and also contains new information concerning entry into the federal market. I provide anecdotes drawn from my forty years of experience in the federal market. Hopefully, the anecdotes and insight provided will help your business make a successful foray into the market.

The war in Iraq continues, the occurrence of natural disasters seems to be on the rise, and federal spending on products and services continues to increase at startling rates. The Democrats are in control of Congress and their agenda is more small-business friendly than that of the Republican administration. Many small businesses have watched the federal market from the sidelines with envy. Why not get off the sidelines and join the game? All you need to figure out is how the game is played. It is not that difficult once you clear away the fog of red tape. See through the haze and win your share of federal business.

Introduction

My company's web site, www.fedmarket.com, is known for presenting the realities of doing business with the federal government. The thought of entering the federal market strikes fear in the hearts of many citizens. Most outsiders view it as a competition dominated by behemoths such as Halliburton and Lockheed Martin. While it is true that the market is dominated by insiders and the red tape involved with the selling in the market can be confusing, none of the barriers to market entry make it impenetrable in any way.

Books on the power of positive thinking appear on all of the bestseller lists. They have one basic message: positive thinking creates focused action. With the power of positive thinking foremost in your mind, you should consider the following:

- The federal market is not more difficult to enter than any other new market. In fact, small businesses which are able to take advantage of federal set-aside programs often find the federal market easier to solve than other markets.

- Some small businesses enter the federal market on a shoe string and grow into very large companies.

- The big federal contractors were new to the market at one point in time.

- Some insiders are mediocre performers yet they continue to grow.

- Knowledge is power and knowing the idiosyncrasies of the market can alleviate the fear of tackling the unknown.

- It only takes one contract (or order) to become an insider.

- Once in the market, you can use your insider status to help your business grow at warp speed.

In order to tap into the federal market, a company must be willing to make the investment necessary to penetrate the market. But this initial investment does not necessarily have to be in the form of dollars. The dollar investment can be minimized with positive energy and focus. We suggest following the steps outlined below in order to maximize your corporate expenditure:

1. Learn what the market is all about first and get rid of the fear of the unknown. Then take advantage of what you know by getting a pre-approved federal price list.

2. Use preference programs to give you a selling edge.

3. Sell in your geographic locale. You would be surprised by the number of federal dollars available in your backyard.

4. Focus on a niche within the market that needs your product or service.

5. Develop a distinguishing message about your strengths.

6. Refuse to accept "no" for an answer. At the same time, don't badger the buyer.

Read on and learn how to crack the market by keeping these six points in mind.

Table of Contents

Chapter 1

The Best Offense is a Good Defense

Outsider Perception: The market is impenetrable.

Reality: Entering the federal market is no different than entering a new segment of the commercial market; it just appears mysterious from the outside.

Lesson: Don't shy away from the federal market. Entering the market can transform your company and it is an effective way to counter a slowing economy.

Background:

The federal market is growing so fast that it's virtually impossible to determine its size. Experts theorize that the federal government spends between $450 million and $500 million annually. The market is unlikely to slow down when one considers the monies spent to combat terrorism, to fund the Iraq war, and to finance the recovery efforts needed after recent natural disasters.

Do you find yourself asking, "Why did our competition win that big federal contract and not us?" You deserve some of the $500 billion being spent annually so go after it. The federal market isn't as mysterious as you might think. Succeeding in the federal arena requires a focused effort up front to unravel the red tape and figure out how the game is played. Consider entering the federal market as a defensive move against a slowing economy. So what if the economy doesn't slow down? You will have increased sales and strengthened your company.

Although deciding to tap into the federal market is generally a smart business strategy, companies often shy away from the prospect. The most prevalent reasons for this are:

1. The apprehension concerning the red tape associated with federal work

2. The perception that the market is a closed one dominated by the big players

3. The misconception that if your business is not located in the nation's capitol, it won't be successful in the federal game

4. The fear that the federal market is completely different from the commercial market

Most of the reasons outlined above boil down to a lack of understanding of the market or a fear of the unknown. With just a little bit of research and the knowledge gleaned from such research, you may find federal business right in your backyard. From a political standpoint, both Congress and the White House favor small businesses because of their importance to the economy. In fact, recent legislation enacted by Congress encourages federal installations to purchase from small business owners. Why shouldn't these customers do business with you?

Trying to understand federal purchasing rules is often like solving a complex jigsaw puzzle. Congress is considering steps to solve the problem but your grandchildren will be running your business by the time we see any meaningful changes in the way federal rules are written. Fear not. There are solutions and this book is just one solution. Consider attending seminars on federal sales run by experts such as those offered by Fedmarket.com. Go in and talk to federal contracting officers located in your region. They can often help to educate companies on how to do business with the federal government. And, if you are lucky, you might even gain a federal client in the process.

Chapter 2

Make the World's Biggest Customer Your Own

Outsider Perception: The federal market is enormous.

Reality: The market is much bigger than you think. In order to enter the market, your sales staff should tackle the federal market as it would any new customer in the commercial setting.

Lesson: The federal market is virtually identical to the commercial market. The major difference is that your business must have a way to close (transact) a deal that it has sold.

Background:

As discussed previously, the federal government spends approximately $500 billion on an annual basis. Half of all federal contracts are awarded through limited competitions or sole-source awards. By any measure, the federal government is the world's biggest and most lucrative customer. Study the federal market and then go after the business in the same way as you do in your current market. If your company qualifies for a small business preference program, it can quickly become a $100 million company if it learns to play the federal game.

What is needed to make the federal government your customer?

1. A unique product or one with a feature that distinguishes it from all of the rest or a demonstrated history of providing exemplary, high-quality services

2. A sales staff member who can focus his or her efforts on federal sales

3. A pre-awarded federal contract which provides for pre-approved pricing for federal agencies

Doing business with the federal government may seem enigmatic on the surface. At its core, it is virtually identical to the commercial market or any other market in which you might be selling. Government red tape makes the process seem daunting but the sales process is the same as the commercial market up to the point where the sale is transacted. In order to actually make a sale to a federal customer, your sales staff must:

1. Identify a federal buyer who is looking for what you sell.

2. Knock on the buyer's door.

3. Weather the buyer's initial reluctance to partner with new companies.

4. Convince the federal buyer that your business will provide value that your competitors can't offer.

Think about it. Don't you have to do all of the foregoing when making a sale to your current customer base? Now for the variance; federal rules require varying degrees of competition before your sale can be transacted. The reality is that in the majority of federal sales transactions, there is little or no competition. Contrary to popular belief, federal purchasing rules allow limited competition and the most successful insiders or experienced federal contractors know how to close their sales within the rules. The rules are different under different circumstances. Determining factors are those such as the dollar amount of the buy or the availability of vendors with a pre-approved price list. So what's the secret? Learn how to play within the federal rules which limit competition.

Finding a federal buyer who needs what you sell can be difficult at first but, after you have some experience in the process, it becomes relatively easy. There are millions of federal end users spread throughout the world upon whom you may call. You may ask, "How do I find end users, the procurement decision makers?" Some use the Internet to painstakingly compile a list of end users. Others monitor Fedbizopps, the federal bid site, to see what contracting officers are buying, or attend government-sponsored procurement conferences.

Identifying federal buyers becomes easier after you win your first federal contract because you can then use your federal customer to help you find others. Federal buyers are happy to give you more contact information once they know and trust you. More detailed information on identifying federal end users can be found in Appendix A.

There is a growing trend in federal procurement offices to transact purchases using pre-approved price list contracts. Approximately 15,000 insiders already have pre-approved price lists. Your company can close your sales quickly—while still following the procurement rules—if you hold this type of contract (e.g., a GSA Schedule contract). When a pre-approved price list is in place, a purchase can be closed quickly because federal procurement rules presume that the competition took place when you negotiated the price list. Later chapters will help to clear up any confusion regarding the level of competition required under the rules.

Chapter 3

Market Research in the Federal Sector

Outsider Perception: The federal government keeps detailed statistics on what it purchases.

Reality: The tracking of federal spending is marginal at best.

Lesson: Do what you can and then apply your "street smarts."

Background:

The size of the federal market is not a particularly meaningful number if only a tiny slice of the market is really available to your company. A janitorial services company in the Chicago area has a limited geographic area in which it can realistically deliver its services. The key questions for this type of company are whether there are federal offices or installations in their locale and do these entities need their services. Once that question is addressed, the next question becomes "How much of the available work is currently held by incumbent contractors and how much of it is new work?" By doing research, your company should be able to target the sources and amount of work available to local vendors. Once the analysis is complete, your business should have a list of federal customers it wants to pursue.

A company selling office supplies has a different set of questions to answer because office supplies can be sold by telephone to virtually any federal customer regardless of his or her location. The critical unanswered questions are:

- Where should our efforts be focused when attempting to sell to a federal customer?

- When and how does price enter into the picture?

- What importance does the customer place on service?

- How difficult is it to replace an entrenched office supply company and how can it be done?

Now we are in the world of what we call "street smarts." Your sales staff will most likely have to get on the telephone to answer these questions. You could test the market by making small sales to federal buyers who use their government credit cards to transact the sales. In the long run, your business will most likely need a pre-approved federal price list in order to compete (such price lists will be discussed in greater detail later).

The federal government's product and service coding system is not detailed enough to make research by product type very meaningful although some raw data is available in the following public contract award databases:

Federal Funding Accountability and Transparency Act (FFATA) Database: FFATA Search Portal

Federal Spending.org Contracts Database: Fedspending.org/fpds

Chapter 4

Become an Insider in the Federal Market

Outsider Perception: The federal market is dominated by insiders.

Reality: A large portion of the federal pie is given to insiders who know how to play the federal sales game.

Lesson: Become an insider by selling in your own backyard with an aggressive sales program.

Background:

Consider becoming an insider and share in the fruits of the world's largest market. Remember, the insiders were on the outside looking in at one point in time and the game is not that tough to play once you understand it. In order to become an insider, you must first understand how competition (or the lack of it) influences how buys are made. Furthermore, your company must hold a direct contract with a federal customer. It only takes one. Having an existing federal contract allows your business to demonstrate, through your partnership with the government, that your product or service provides value to the federal buyer or end user. This partnership becomes the path of least resistance. It is the path that minimizes the federal buyer's risk and the path that allows buyers to obtain what they want quickly and efficiently. As in the commercial market, federal buyers go with the proven vendor. Think about it. You do the same thing when purchasing goods or services.

You may be saying to yourself, "This sounds easy. So, what's the catch?" Landing the first contract requires the establishment of a business relationship with the buyer and you probably don't have one. Any sales person will tell you getting through the glass wall to a new customer can be a formidable task; the potential customer most likely already has business partners and may not realize that she needs you. But getting through the glass wall is not any more difficult than selling to a new commercial customer.

Don't go to the Washington, D.C. area initially. There are too many entrenched insiders playing there. Find federal buyers in your locale or region. You will be dumbfounded by the volume of federal work to be found in your immediate geographic area. Use federal directories published by military bases, federal agency web sites, and your local blue pages (which list federal telephone numbers and addresses).

Military bases and the federal installations and offices located outside of Washington, D.C., prefer to buy locally. If you were a federal procurement officer, you would probably prefer to buy a dozen digital cameras from a local photo shop rather than a national chain. You would have better access to service and it is the politically correct thing to do. Natural disasters and the threat of terrorism have also resulted in new, more flexible purchasing rules that allow sole-source buys under emergency situations and specify that preference should be given to local sources for products and services.

Ask for introductions to federal buyers through your current network of existing customers, neighbors, fellow church goers and the like. Attend local chamber of commerce events, business conferences and industry events. Attend local or regional business opportunity conferences held by federal agencies. Make cold calls beginning with the contracting offices for those federal agencies in your area.

In short, selling in the federal market is just like selling in the commercial market. People buy, not agencies, and most sales are based on the development of strong relationships with federal buyers. The two markets diverge when it comes to closing the sale you have made with the buyer. Market characteristics and how they impact closing the federal sale will be the subject of the next two chapters.

Chapter 5

Competition and Price Sensitivity in the Federal Market

Outsider Perception: The federal market is open and competitive.

Reality: Competition does take place but, for most transactions, it is limited so that purchases can be made quickly and at reasonable cost to the taxpayer.

Lesson: Learn how purchases are made under the rules for limited competition and use this knowledge to win business.

Background:

It is a fallacy that federal purchases are made only after full and open competition takes place. Competition may or may not occur but, when it does, it is usually limited. In most instances, a company is not going to win a federal bid opportunity it stumbled onto online. The truth is that your competitors met with the federal buyers long before the opportunity was publicly announced and the federal buyer already has one or more companies in mind. Federal bureaucrats do not like to admit this reality because they are tasked with the responsibility of getting the best value for the American taxpayer. The reality is that federal purchasing rules not only allow federal buyers to meet with vendors prior to the announcement of a public bid but the rules actually encourage it. How else would a federal buyer assess the value of proffered products and services?

On the surface, this reality may seem discouraging. On the other hand, those companies with aggressive salespeople and a distinct message should have no problem becoming one of the few companies being considered for a contract or order. Learn how to limit competition and become one of the chosen few. Treat the market just like your current market and go after federal end users.

A second myth is that federal buying decisions are made based solely on price considerations. Once again, the federal market is like the commercial market in that you can sell based on value rather than on price. And best value is defined broadly in federal purchasing rules. My father used to say, "Son, you get what you pay for." While it is true that, at one point in time, federal government buyers made purchasing decisions based primarily on price, the government has modernized its regulations to allow buying decisions based on best value.

Service prices are inherently difficult to value. Which heart surgeon would you like to have operate on you? They may all charge close to the same rates but price may not be as big a factor as the surgeon's experience and skill. It really isn't any different than trying to select a computer programmer. A computer programmer who charges $80.00 per hour may churn out double the work than one who is billed at $120.00 an hour. It is far easier to determine the value of offered services if your organization has worked with the company in the past.

In contrast, price is a much bigger consideration when commodities are purchased. Copy paper and paper clips are fairly standard items no matter where you buy them. In fact, price may be the only factor if you are buying in high volume.

As a taxpayer, you should be happy that best value can now be considered. As a sales person, it's an answer to your prayers. It gives government buyers the latitude to use their judgment and the sales person the opportunity to sell quality, features, benefits, results, and past performance. All of these factors can be considered in determining best value. Making direct sales calls to government buyers will pay off in the long run as long as you are selling quality and value.

Chapter 6

Are Federal Bids Wired?

Outsider Perception: Most federal bids are wired for insiders like Halliburton.

Reality: The term "wired" is too strong a word. Companies which pre-sell federal opportunities are in a favored position.

Lesson: Identify federal opportunities early, sell your solution, and place yourself in a favored position.

Background:

Many members of the American public believe that federal bids are "wired," implying that the bid is set up or rigged to favor a particular company. Although public bids are not wired in the truest sense of the word, the reality is that decision makers may favor the incumbent contractor or one or more companies that have done the following:

- Convinced the end user, through pre-selling, that they offer a superior product or service

- Taken the time to get to know the agency and the specific requirements of the procurement through pre-selling or through having done prior work for the agency

- Demonstrated in previous contracts with an agency that they are proven performers

- Proven to the agency, through references from other customers, that they are a reputable vendor

Purchases made through public bids represent a relatively small percentage of buys made in the federal market. More often, purchases are made through pre-approved price list contracts or modifications to existing federal contracts.

An opportunity may be put out for public bid if:

- The agency knows a number of companies have been aggressively pre-selling the opportunity and the only option, from a political standpoint, is to conduct a public bid.

- The project is large and highly visible.

- The vendor the agency wants to work with doesn't have a pre-approved price list and there isn't a prime contractor available to use as a conduit.

- The contract that was originally bid publicly comes up for renewal.

- The agency needs to pad its public bid numbers.

- The agency truly doesn't have a vendor pre-selected (yes, this happens on occasion).

Don't bid on a public procurement if you haven't done significant advance research. A bidder must have all of the background information in order to understand the nuances of the deal. There is always a back story and the vendor that eventually wins the contract will have uncovered all of the intelligence well in advance of the posting of the bid.

Chapter 7

Fundamentals of Federal Contracting

Outsider Perception: In order to participate in the federal market, you must accept the mountains of red tape that come with handling such business.

Reality: The red tape is not so onerous that it should scare your business away from participating in the federal arena.

Lesson: Don't let the red tape scare you. It consists of a series of administrative tasks which, although tedious, can be easily tackled.

Background:

Many people lose sight of the fact that doing business with the federal government is done according to a contract. A federal contract is nothing more than an agreement between your company and the federal government under which your business agrees to provide a product or service in accordance with the terms of the document. The contract dictates the parameters of the deal and is the underlying basis for your relationship with the customer. Federal contracts contain countless pages of boilerplate language and convoluted clauses. Don't let the terms of the contract scare you—the contract is only onerous on the surface. Pick out the wheat from the chaff and perform as you would with your commercial customers. Go to the contract when issues arise and let the contract dictate how disputes are resolved or an issue should be addressed.

The role of the federal contracting officer is central in the federal purchasing process. Except for credit card purchases, the contracting officer is the person authorized to execute federal contracts and orders. This means that only a person who is formally designated as a contracting officer can solicit proposals, negotiate, award (sign), and change (modify) contracts on behalf of the U.S. government. The contracting officer is charged with ensuring that, as required under the Federal Acquisition Regulation, the required amount of competition occurs. To say the least, the procurement rules are complex and long.

The contracting officer has considerable latitude in determining how a buy is made and can consider subjective factors in determining how to close a sale. "Factors" is the operative word here. Factors that can affect the contracting officer's final decision include the dollar amount of the buy, when the product or service is needed, the type of businesses competing, the qualifications of the bidders and more.

When commodities such as office supplies are purchased, contracting officers are often the sole decision makers in determining who gets the business. In contrast, the federal end user is the person consuming or using what you sell. They buy to support their program or operational responsibilities and make the final purchasing decisions concerning the acquisition of more complex products and professional services. An end user makes procurement decisions based on opinions they have formed from meetings or telephone discussions with corporate sales people and through their experience in working with a particular company in the past.

End users often find themselves in conflict with contracting officers. They are averse to taking risks and, as most of us do, they generally protect their self interest. Furthermore, end users usually want what is needed quickly and without hassle. The purchasing process is often slowed down by contracting officers who are charged with ensuring that the rules are being followed. Because a contracting officer cannot realistically monitor a particular company's performance or make substantive decisions regarding a particular product or service's value, he or she will delegate these responsibilities to the end user.

Think of the end user and contracting officers as partners. Then think of yourself as the third partner in the deal who has been entrusted with the responsibility of performing and delivering under the terms of the contract. This may seem trite but your key to success will be constant (sometimes daily) communication with both government partners. They want to know and trust their business partner. This is why it is critical that you become a partner (or an insider) and gain this trust.

Chapter 8

Making a Federal Sale

Outsider Perception: Federal agencies order products and services only from their favored vendors.

Reality: People buy—not agencies—and favored vendors have to sell to government buyers just as any other company hoping to do business with the federal government.

Lesson: In the federal market, products and services are sold by people to people. You must sell an end user first and then close the sale within the government's purchasing rules.

Background:

Contrary to popular belief, people buy in the federal market, not agencies. The best way to make a federal sale is to contact a buyer through a direct sales call. Making direct sales in the federal market can be challenging but the truth is that such sales calls are difficult in any market. The federal dollars are there to be made if you make a determination to go after them. Don't let your inexperience in the market deter you from going forward.

The primary difference with the federal market is that it is critical that you have a way to close the sale. And, of course, it is more difficult to find the end users who buy what you sell because you are new to the market. Although rules and regulations often tie a government buyer's hands, they don't turn the buyer into a robot. Federal buyers are people with the same general motivations and inclinations we all have, rules or no rules. Federal end users buy from vendors they know and trust. The government employee's success and future promotions depend on the value of the products and services they buy and, because of that, they want to be assured that their vendors will perform well. The people in the federal sales process and their motivations are discussed more fully in Appendix B.

It's not just about getting the best deal for the taxpayer. Although certainly a factor, "taxpayer protection" is often a fuzzy, nebulous concept. The reality is that the federal buyer wants to get the deal that works best for him and his superiors. From a federal buyer's perspective, a good deal is one in which risk is minimized.

Most federal sales, like commercial sales, start with a customer relationship. To be successful in the market, you must consider the entire sales cycle as a business process. Many outsiders think that they can jump into the middle of the process. Because the federal government publicizes its bidding opportunities at a central web site, companies hoping to win business with the government think they can simply conduct a search and pick and choose projects to bid on. As you may have surmised, jumping in the middle doesn't work. In order to be successful in the federal market, your sales staff must (i) make direct sales calls to establish trust relationships with end users, and (ii) learn to play the "close the sale" game.

How many vendors will be selling the same opportunity? It depends on both the size and type of opportunity. The level of competition increases proportionately with the size (in terms of dollars) of the contract to be awarded. Some vendors will have the opportunity on their wish list but will burn out in the proposal-writing phase. Others may want to bid but simply haven't laid enough groundwork to be serious contenders. Those who are most likely to succeed will be the vendors who are dead serious, focused, have a relationship with the end user and the willingness to spend the time and money it takes to win a bid opportunity. The amount of competition also depends on the risk perceived by the end user. The question to be addressed is whether the federal officials involved believe there is a practical and economical solution to their problem. The more uncertainty, the more likely it is that the procurement will be competitive.

Determining a customer's pain is crucial to success. You must delve in and focus on the customer, not on what you are selling. To "create a solution," the vendor needs to fully understand the customer's problem. Once your company understand the customer's needs or issues, your staff must craft a solution and educate the customer about why your solution is the answer to his problem. This step is what distinguishes your business from all of the thousands of competitors out there.

Finally, the third step is to "make it easy." Vendors must make it painless for the end user or contracting officer to choose their product or service. Companies make it easy for procurement officials by obtaining pre-approved price lists such as a GSA Schedule contract. Schedule contracts make the procurement officer's job much easier because the use of a Schedule vendor dramatically reduces the contracting officer's paperwork. More importantly, a purchase made through a Schedule vendor can be accomplished much faster than through a public procurement. The process is called "sole or limited source" since a procurement official can award the business with little or no competition based on the fact that the source (or vendor) has a pre-approved federal pricelist for its product or service. When a government purchase is made through a GSA Schedule contract, it is assumed that full and open competition has taken place and, accordingly, the need for a public procurement no longer exists.

The ability to close a deal is the key. In fact, it separates the insiders from the newcomers. A federal sale must be closed through a procedure or contractual mechanism that is consistent with the rules for competition in the public sector. The closing procedure is normally dictated and implemented by the contracting officer unless the purchase is a small one made with a federal credit card. The closing process is discussed in more detail in the next chapter.

Chapter 9

Closing a Federal Sale

Outsider Perception: Federal sales opportunities are almost always announced through public bids which are open to all. Federal buyers then evaluate vendor responses and pick the eventual winner.

Reality: Federal sales are closed (transacted) in a number of ways and the least preferable way is through a public bid.

Lesson: Learn the ways sales are closed and use the most appropriate way to your advantage.

Background:

Closing a sale means getting the order, winning the contract, or collecting the money (as in the case of a credit card purchase). Closing a federal sale is where the rubber hits the road; how it's done is the fundamental difference between the federal and commercial markets. Experienced federal contractors know how to close their sales. They also know the "closing rules"—and the rules are not that puzzling once you boil them down to their bare essence. Outsiders mistakenly believe that federal agencies have to open an opportunity to all who want to bid. As previously discussed, this is a fallacy.

As public policy dictates, federal contracting officers must strictly follow the procurement rules. When the government has a need for a complex product or a service, the federal end user generally meets with one or more vendors to obtain information about the features and benefits of a particular product or service and to get a handle on the past performance or experience of the company making the offering to the government.

The end user then meets with the contracting officer to discuss the issues concerning the procurement.

The contracting officer will then close the deal using the quickest method allowed under the rules. This is where the process becomes complex. The contracting officer may or may not seek additional competitors depending on the amount of money involved and whether or not the companies involved have pre-approved price lists.

The following summarizes the methods in which a federal purchase can be closed or transacted:

- By a government credit card buy (the quickest and simplest method)

- By the issuance of a purchase order for amounts under $100,000; the federal purchaser must first obtain at least two quotes (relatively simple)

- By the issuance of a public bid (a long, lengthy, and expensive process which is usually avoided if possible)

- Through a contract that allows the government to purchase from a select list of companies which have pre-approved price lists (e.g., a GSA Schedule contract)

- Through a subcontract with a prime contractor that already has a federal contract

- Through a subcontract with a "preferred" small business with which the government can contract quickly and with limited or no competition (e.g., a small disadvantaged business, Alaskan Native Corporation, etc.)

- Keep in mind that a contracting officer has broad authority in determining how the purchase can be made as long as the buy is made within the purchasing rules. The manner in which a purchase is completed usually depends on the size of the transaction. More information about the differing sizes of transactions and purchasing procedures will be presented in upcoming chapters.

Chapter 10

Start with the Credit Card and Quick Buy Markets for Smaller Transactions

Outsider Perception: Federal purchases are made the same way regardless of the amount of money involved.

Reality: The rules regarding credit card purchases and quick buys make it easy to do business in the federal market for transactions under $100,000.

Lesson: Use the rules concerning credit card purchases and quick buys to your advantage. Federal buyers located outside of the Washington, DC, Beltway use these procedures extensively to do business with local small businesses.

Background:

The uninitiated do not realize how easy it is to do business in the under-$100,000 segment of the federal market. Federal purchases of less than $100,000 are theoretically set aside for small businesses (although there is a current dispute between the Small Business Administration and GSA regarding whether this is indeed true). Think about it. Many small businesses across the country would not consider a $99,000 sale insignificant.

The federal small buy market is divided into two sectors. They are as follows:

Credit Card Single-Source Purchases

A federal buyer can place orders of less than $3,000 using a government credit card. Such orders can be placed without the necessity for competition and with a company of the buyer's choice. These buys are usually made by end users and can be made without a contracting officer's involvement.

The following example demonstrates how a credit card purchase may transpire. Let's assume that a federal end user's hard drive crashes. He has an immediate need for a replacement so he buys a new computer by credit card from a local retailer. Under this scenario, the end user is up and running in a matter of hours. How much closer to the commercial market can you get?

If the purchase is made in support of a contingency operation (in simple terms, a purchase made for military purposes during a time of war or natural disaster), or to facilitate a defense against terrorism, the credit card limits increase to $15,000 for purchases made inside the United Sates and $25,000 for buys outside the United States.

Quick Buys from $3,000 to $100,000

Similar rules also apply to orders of between $3,000 and $100,000 but the procedures are slightly more stringent. We call such transactions "quick buys." In the federal vernacular, the procedures which apply to quick buys are called "simplified acquisition procedures." Quick buys can be made after obtaining quotes (by fax, email, or orally) from a minimum of two sources. If the purchase supports a contingency operation or is necessary to facilitate a defense against terrorism, the quick buy limit increases to $250,000 for purchases made within the United Sates and $1 million for buys outside the United States.

National Emergency Procedures

Federal purchasing rules were recently relaxed for purchases made in response to emergencies or natural disasters. The new rules allow contracting officers to limit the use of full and open competition when the President has made a declaration of emergency under the Robert T. Stafford Disaster Relief and Emergency Assistance Act.

In this scenario, contracting officers may set aside opportunities for companies located or doing business primarily in the area affected by the disaster or emergency. In essence, the new legislation allows contracting officers to make sole-source purchases from companies located within areas affected by disaster without Congress coming down on them for rule violations. Keep in mind that the President must make a formal declaration first.

Chapter 11

Consider Starting as a Subcontractor to a Prime

Outsider Perception: Most federal business is conducted with direct contracts between the end user and the vendor.

Reality: A large amount of federal business is done through commercial subcontracts with federal prime contractors.

Lesson: Subcontracting is a valid way to close a sale when your business doesn't have another method to do so.

Background:

Companies that don't have pre-approved federal price lists usually have to start out as a subcontractor to a company that already has a contract with the federal agency. These insiders are commonly called "prime contractors." Assuming they want to do business with you, contracting officers can elect to have one of their existing prime contractors execute a subcontract with your business as a way to close a deal under the rules. For example, your company could sell a product or service to an end user at a particular agency and the agency may decide that the best way to close your sale is through a subcontract with a trusted prime contractor (as opposed to going through a lengthy and expensive public bid process).

The contracting officer may also elect to put you in contact with a small business that holds a preference certification (such as a Section 8(a) small disadvantaged business certification) because the government can sole source to this type of business if the transaction is under $3 million. Under this scenario, a new contract would be executed with the certified small business and your company would become a subcontractor under the new preference contract. Convoluted as it may sound, many federal sales are closed using commercial subcontracts.

Subcontracting is a valid way to close a sale but it has drawbacks. The primary drawback is that a subcontract with a prime contractor doesn't give you that critical first step toward achieving insider status. When acting as a subcontractor, you do not have a contract with the federal government. Instead your business has a commercial contract with the prime contractor. The prime contractor controls your company's prices, your sales growth, and your destiny with the federal customer. A savvy prime contractor also insulates the federal customer from its subcontractors so the subcontractors never really achieve insider status.

Chapter 12

Selling Directly to Prime Contractors

Outsider Perception: Selling products, services, and solutions to a federal prime contractor is easier than selling directly to the federal government.

Reality: Selling products, services, and solutions to a prime contractor can be as frustrating as selling directly to federal agencies.

Lesson: You must sell your products and services to prime contractors in the same way you would to your prospective federal customers.

Background:

Many small businesses start out in the federal market by serving as subcontractors to federal prime contractors. These companies are forced to do so because they don't have ways to close their sales. In fact, most small businesses don't know about pre-approved price list contracts until they have been in the game for six months or more.

Prime contractors are required by law to subcontract a percentage of their federal work to various types of small businesses (e.g., small disadvantaged businesses, veteran-owned small businesses, women-owned small businesses, and the like). This is a major element in the federal government's small business advocacy program and it works. Most people believe that mandatory subcontracting is a good approach but small businesses beware. There is an inherent flaw in the system in that prime contractors agree on paper to use good faith efforts to use small businesses but do not do so in practice. The way to keep the prime contractors honest is to force the prime contractor to sign an airtight teaming agreement which obligates the prime contractor to send small companies the work outlined in the bid proposal.

Selling services and solutions to a prime contractor can be as frustrating as selling directly to federal agencies. The primes usually have a plethora of small businesses under their umbrella, and making cold calls to a prime contractor is like any other cold call. Your first task is to find the key decision makers in the organization and most are buried deep within the inner layers of the prime's bureaucracy.

If your primary contact directs you to the prime contractor's Diversity Department or Small Business Advocacy Group, you have been given the kiss of death. These departments will ask you to submit your capabilities statement for entry into their small business capabilities database. Your proffered statement will most probably wind up in the department head's circular file and it is not likely that your business will hear back from that prime.

In contrast, there may be limited scenarios under which the prime contractor will welcome you with open arms. They are as follows:

Your sales staff has sold your company's services to an end user at a military base near your hometown. The end user wants to do business with your company and has money to spend. You don't have a closing mechanism, such as a GSA Schedule contract, so the base referred you to the contract manager for their favorite prime contractor. Under this scenario, the prime will embrace your company because you have brought an unforeseen opportunity to its attention and also because it will make a handsome profit by marking up your fees and costs.

The two other situations in which your company may make successful inroads with a prime are if your company has a unique capability that the prime contractor needs and can't find elsewhere or if someone in your network of contacts knows a decision maker in the prime contractor's organization and has provided an excellent reference for your company.

Beginning as a subcontractor to a prime is a good way to get your foot in the door because it is fast and relatively painless. As mentioned previously, the major drawbacks are that the prime contractor will try to insulate your company from the customer, take credit for your staff's superior performance, and attempt to grab the bulk of any new work you uncover.

Chapter 13

Pre-approved Government Price Lists

Outsider Perception: Federal work is awarded only after a lengthy public bid process takes place.

Reality: A great deal of federal business is conducted through companies with "pre-approved federal price lists" rather than through the public bid route.

Lesson: In order to compete, you must get one of the aforementioned pre-approved federal price lists.

Background:

We have previously discussed how closing a federal sale is different than closing a sale in the commercial market. Federal sales must be closed under federal purchasing rules which most often require that some type of competition take place. Established federal contractors usually close their sales using pre-approved federal price lists. These special contracts are awarded to companies that submit an offer for consideration and are deemed of merit by GSA. The contracts reduce, and sometimes eliminate, competition because sales opportunities are offered to only the companies holding the contracts.

The best pre-approved price list contracts for small businesses are GSA Schedule contracts. To get a GSA Schedule contract, you must have sold your offered product or service to others first. As a result, GSA Schedules have limitations for start-ups and for companies hoping to offer new or beta products. In spite of these limitations, Schedule contracts are ideal for small businesses because they are open to all qualified businesses.

In the simplest terms, GSA Schedule contracts make your company's products and services available to any federal buyer at prices pre-negotiated with the federal government. Product prices are negotiated on a unit basis; service prices are negotiated on an hourly basis. In essence, the Schedule contract is a pre-negotiated federal price list that can be used by federal buyers to make purchases from your business quickly and with limited paperwork or red tape.

The following is an example of how a GSA Schedule sale is transacted. Let's assume you run a small office supply business located near a military base. Your sales staff has been calling on the base for an extended period of time but has not yet had success. In fact, the base has been using the same large office supply company for years and is reluctant to change this practice. It is late August and it appears that the base's printing center will have around $300,000 remaining in its annual budget. Furthermore, the government's fiscal year ends on September 30th and the printing center doesn't want the $300,000 to go unspent (under the axiom "use it or lose it"). The base's management directs its procurement staff to send work to small businesses so that the base meets its annual small business participation goals.

The printing center manager calls and asks if your company can deliver 10,000 cases of multi-purpose copy paper to the base for the sum of $300,000. Because he is familiar with the costs associated with office supplies, the manager knows that $30 a case is a fair price for a high-volume order. He tells your sales person that the base has several thousand cases in inventory but it can always use copy paper and that the $300,000 needs to be spent by September 30th. He further states that you can take your time in delivering the product since the base's storeroom is fairly full at this point. The center manager then says, "I hope you have a GSA Schedule contract because we do not have time for a public procurement and this buy needs to be inked ASAP." Thankfully, your company does indeed hold a GSA Schedule contract for office supplies and your pre-approved price for the product in question is $36 per case. Knowing that GSA allows a Schedule contractor to agree to pricing that is lower than your awarded GSA pricing—especially in instances in which a high-volume order is involved—you strike a deal. Imagine if your business had not held a Schedule contract. The opportunity would have slipped through your hands.

To summarize, a GSA Schedule contract may be the only way that a small business can compete with the larger, more experienced federal contractors. You should focus your efforts immediately on getting on the GSA Schedule so that you can close deals quickly and efficiently.

Chapter 14

Getting a Pre-approved Federal Price List for Your Company

Outsider Perception: Doing federal business requires that you jump through bureaucratic hoops.

Reality: In order to get a pre-approved federal price list, your company must jump through several hoops.

Lesson: Although the process is tedious and often painstakingly slow, take the plunge and work towards getting your pre-approved federal price list.

Background:

Previous chapters have repeatedly mentioned that having pre-approved federal prices is critical to sales success. The best type of pre-approved price contracts for small businesses is a GSA Schedule contract. A Schedule contract is ideal for small businesses because companies can apply for them at any time and they are open to all qualified businesses. Companies should apply for a GSA Schedule contract immediately upon deciding to enter the federal market.

Getting pre-approved federal prices requires considerable red tape. Companies submitting a GSA Schedule proposal must, among other things, describe their corporate experience (if offering services), provide their commercial prices for the offered product or service, and disclose their commercial discounting practices. Because of the complexity of the task, an entire industry has emerged devoted to helping companies get through the application process. Companies can complete GSA Schedule proposals on their own provided they have a person with government contracting experience or they have a senior financial person with lots of time and the tenacity of a pit bull.

Although GSA Schedule applications are tedious, the critical components of your company's GSA offer are the disclosures concerning your commercial pricing and the level to which you have discounted off your commercial prices. GSA uses these commercial discounting disclosures to seek the lowest price you have offered others. The American taxpayer should be pleased that GSA contracting officers have this mandate.

Those GSA Schedule solicitations which apply to services (in contrast to products) require that a company demonstrate that it has the background or corporate experience necessary to provide the services it is offering to the government. In some instances, a company must have been in business for two or three years in order to be considered. This requirement obviously presents a problem to new companies that have no corporate experience to draw upon. However, select GSA solicitations allow a company offering services to proffer the experience of management with a previous employer as the corporate experience required under that Schedule's solicitation. Start-ups hoping to offer products to GSA also face a hurdle because GSA requires that a company submitting an offer prove that it has sold the product in the commercial marketplace. In spite of the challenges described above, it is well worth your company's time and effort to work towards getting on a Schedule contract.

More information on GSA Schedule contracts is presented in Appendix C.

Chapter 15

Small Business Preference Programs

Outsider Perception: The federal government likes to do business with small businesses.

Reality: Federal buyers need incentives to convince them to contract with small businesses because the buyers perceive that there's more risk associated with small companies.

Lesson: If available to your company, use any and all small business preference programs to help you close business with the government.

Background:

Federal purchases of less than $100,000 are, in most instances, set aside for small businesses. This program helps small businesses considerably, but keep in mind that there is competition for set-asides. Just because your company qualifies for a particular preference program doesn't mean your work is done; your sales staff must still pre-sell these opportunities rather than bid on them blindly.

A similar program requires that federal prime contractors subcontract a percentage of their federal contracts in excess of $550,000 to small businesses. Like set-asides, this program is designed to help small businesses. However, your company still must sell itself to a federal buyer before it will be considered as a subcontractor. Or you have to become a favorite in a prime contractor's stable of small businesses—a process which requires that you either have experience working with that prime or a recommendation from a reputable, highly-placed source.

It is not uncommon for a large prime contractor to use small business programs as a way to close a federal sale. Under this scenario, the prime contractor becomes a subcontractor to the small business with preference status. The terms of the federal contract will most likely specify that at least 50% of the contract's personnel costs must be spent on work performed by employees of the prime contractor (the small business) or personnel of other small businesses. This stipulation is in place to keep prime contractors from using small businesses and preference programs as fronts when closing sales. Large prime contractors may legally participate in small business preference contracts as long as they closely adhere to this stipulation. Detractors say that in spite of the 50% rule, the small business is still a front for a large business. In the final analysis, the practice works in favor of small businesses so the rules are not likely to change.

The most significant small business programs are the "preference programs" for special types of small businesses. These are the programs that have the greatest potential to rapidly and dramatically increase the sales of a small business. The major preference programs are for (i) small disadvantaged businesses, (ii) service-disabled veteran-owned small businesses, and (iii) small businesses operating in historically underutilized business zones (HUBZones). These programs allow sole-source awards for contracts under $3 million. Such programs give businesses that qualify a significant edge and these programs have been used to build multi-million dollar companies. Qualification requirements for these programs are available at the SBA web site.

It goes without saying that you should jump on these bandwagons if you qualify. The qualification requirements are very specific and should be carefully researched. In the case of small disadvantaged businesses hoping for an 8(a) certification, an actual application for certification must be filed with the SBA. The application is less tedious than that for a GSA Schedule contract and companies, including ours, will assist you in completing the application.

Chapter 16

Distinguishing Messages Win in the Federal Market

Outsider Perception: Selling to the federal government is more difficult than selling to commercial counterparts.

Reality: It is and it isn't. Although the process is the same in both markets, your sales pitch to federal buyers must be more thorough and effective due to the level of competition your business is facing.

Lesson: Develop a distinguishing message to get through federal doors and establish personal relationships with buyers.

Background:

Everyone thinks their competitors are worthless and that they alone have the best product or service known to man. Federal end users have heard "we are the best" so many times that the pitch generally falls on deaf ears. End users want to hear simple facts backed with evidence. Because they have hundreds or thousands of vendors barraging them with messages, you have to have a sales pitch that distinguishes you from the rest. Offer "green" products. Consider having a past federal customer contact the end user to provide a reference.

Distinguish yourself through your initial message to the customer. Federal buyers are like any other buyers in that they want to talk with only those companies that sell what they need. You need a distinguishing message to get through the glass wall encountered by all sales people, commercial or federal. Your message should not be delivered via a link to a web site or a glossy brochure. Such tactics don't work in today's market. Both give the immediate impression that you don't want to take the time to determine what the federal purchaser needs. The message delivered must cut to the heart of the customer's problem. The sales pitch must be individually tailored to the federal buyer's specific needs. Otherwise, it will be quickly cast aside or dismissed.

The following examples show how a message can be crafted to meet the needs of the customer. Let's assume you are an office supply vendor and your headquarters are located near a military base. How do you distinguish your company from the numerous other players in your market? Your message to the base's procurement officer should stress the service you provide in conjunction with the sale of your products. Consider the following sales pitches:

1. "We have a GSA Schedule contract which, by the way, will result in a substantial reduction in paperwork for you. We stock everything you need and can have it at your delivery points within an hour."

2. "If you have problems with a particular product, it will be replaced within three hours."

3. "If you need anything beyond what we sell, we will find it and include it in your order."

4. "Our sales staff and management will be available 24/7, and we will give you our personal cell phone numbers to contact us should the need arise."

Professional services are inherently more difficult for buyers to evaluate because their value is intangible. Your message concerning the types of services your company is capable of providing might be:

1. "We are experts in the subject matter required for your solution and we have enclosed a list of references for your perusal."

2. "We understand your needs and the solicitation's requirements because we have solved similar problems. Brief descriptions of our previous solutions are attached."

3. "Attached is the resume for our proposed project manager."

4. "Here's my cell phone number and I am available 24/7."

5. "I will call you to set up a meeting to discuss our proposed solution."

Consider using any or all of the above suggestions as part of your sales pitch. Deliver it by email and follow up with a personal sales call. Better yet, deliver your message in person and take someone along with you who knows the customer.

Chapter 17

Selling to Federal Agencies Located in Your Backyard

Outsider Perception: All federal business is done inside the Washington Beltway.

Reality: False. More than $250 billion is spent by federal installations and agencies located outside of the nation's capitol.

Lesson: Identify the federal agencies and installations located in your region and sell aggressively to these potential customers.

Background:

Most people are unaware that the federal government spends more than $250 billion on projects located outside of the Washington, DC, metropolitan area. In fact, the federal government's buying power extends across the United States and even worldwide. Some of this money may be spent at military bases or other government installations in your state. You would probably be shocked to discover how much federal business is conducted within 100 miles of your office. Federal officials prefer to work with small businesses located near them since doing so is sound policy from a political and practical standpoint.

Small businesses located within the Washington, DC, metropolitan area do reasonably well because of the vast amounts of money available for contracts in the region. However, the abundance of contract opportunities is offset by the level of competition. The Washington area is home to the very largest prime contractors and small businesses are playing in their backyard. Small businesses hoping to win federal business near the

Beltway must learn to play nice with the large primes or they run the risk of being shut out of the market.

Many small businesses emerge and prosper by staying close to home where the competition is not as intense. There are countless federal facilities located throughout the U.S. and overseas. Such facilities include military bases, research centers, Veterans Administration and military hospitals, and regional offices of various federal agencies. Use your local blue page telephone directory or scroll through the federal agency web sites to locate contact information.

Federal facilities located outside of the Beltway prefer, for political and social reasons, to work with local companies. Local businesses are also perceived by federal officials to be more cognizant of delivering value. It is not uncommon for a small business owner to meet an end user from a local federal facility at a social occasion or at a networking event. He or she can then turn the contact into a business relationship and ultimately a sale.

Take out a local map and draw a circle around your office's location. Contact the federal installations located within the circle. Use the following links to help you find local federal sales opportunities:

General agency searches: USA.gov (the official federal web portal)

For federal offices in your area:

- Federal Telephone Directories; go to Google to access the Federal Citizen Information Center, National Contact Center directories.

- Local blue pages in telephone directories for your area.

- Locate a Military Base: Military.com Installation Guide

- Federal Funded Research and Development Centers: Master Government List of Federally Funded R&D Centers

- Veterans Administration Hospitals: Department of Veterans Affairs Facilities Locator & Directory

- Federal contract award databases: Same award data, different free sites

- Federal Funding Accountability and Transparency Act (FFATA) Database: FFATA Search Portal

- Federal Spending.org Contracts Database: Fedspending.org/fpds

The 2007 California wildfires provide a good example of the use of federal emergency procurement rules and their effect on local businesses. Because a federal emergency was formally declared for Southern California, FEMA was able to buy food, water, tools, and shelters on a sole source basis from local California companies. Did FEMA buy from you? A large number of local businesses in that region were most likely unaware that the emergency procurement rules went into effect. Those companies that were in the know had a real chance to substantially increase their federal business and help out in the disaster relief efforts.

Knowing the rules for disaster purchasing is step one. The second step is to get a pre-approved federal price list. The third step is to let FEMA officials, both in Washington and in your region, know in advance that you have a GSA Schedule contract and the products or services your business can provide in the event of an emergency. Remember that FEMA officials do not necessarily have to buy locally so you can play the game even if your company is not located within the disaster area (particularly if you have an emergency-related product or service).

Chapter 18

Getting Started in Federal Sales

Outsider Perception: Getting your company's federal sales initiative started is an administrative and logistical nightmare.

Reality: The process isn't as bad as you may have heard.

Lesson: Don't let start-up costs and red tape deter your company from entering the federal market.

Background:

We are frequently asked, "What procedures should be followed by small businesses eager to participate in the federal market?" The answer to this question is that a small business should implement an aggressive federal sales program and simultaneously work toward obtaining a GSA Schedule contract. The latter should be of highest priority. A Schedule contract is the only practical way a small business can realistically compete with the fat cats.

What do you do while you are preparing your GSA Schedule offer or are waiting for a submitted offer to be evaluated? The offer evaluation process can take three to nine months so you have plenty of time to do other things. We suggest that your company undertake the following steps:

First and foremost, your company should put a federal sales program in place. Instruct your sales staff to concentrate their efforts on selling directly to federal end users. Do this on Day 1. Provided your business qualifies, submit your 8(a) application to the SBA. Acquiring the 8(a) small disadvantaged business certification is essential for qualified businesses.

The application should be filed within 30 days of instituting your federal sales program.

Contact prime contractors with the goal of working with them as a subcontractor. Close sales using credit card transactions (those under $3,000) or purchase-order transactions (those of less than $100,000) to get your foot in the door. For opportunities that exceed $100,000, inform the federal customer that you are working on your GSA Schedule offer or that it has been submitted and it is in the evaluation stage. Larger deals often take six to twelve months to sell, so your GSA Schedule contract could be awarded by the time your company is ready to close the deal. If your Schedule contract hasn't been awarded by the time your customer is ready to seal the deal, knock on the door of the prime contractor serving the agency and use them to help you win the contract.

Even if your organization fits within the parameters of one of the small business preference programs, approach selling to the government as if you didn't have such a status. Sell aggressively and effectively. Then use your preference edge to help close the deal. Get started today. It helps if you can find someone to pave the way. The best candidate would be someone, such as a business partner or personal friend, who has a federal customer. Government small business specialists or members of Congress are usually not the best candidates to lend assistance. The government gives the impression that it will pave the way for small businesses. Although federal buyers need to contract with small businesses, they are reluctant to do so if they don't have past experience with those vendors. Although it certainly can't hurt to ask agencies like the Small Business Administration, contracting officers, or even your Congressperson for help, you need to have a realistic view of what assistance might be forthcoming. More importantly, you cannot rely on them to make sales calls for you. Counting on the government for help can divert you from making critical, direct sales calls. Don't get sidetracked by thinking that others will sell for you.

Chapter 19

Don't Get Caught Up in Red Tape

Outsider Perception: Red tape is the biggest barrier to entering the federal market.

Reality: The red tape is not as bad as it seems from the outside.

Lesson: Don't let the red tape deter you from cracking the federal market.

Background:

Encountering mountains of red tape is an inevitable consequence of doing business with the federal government. You will be required to register with various federal web sites (such as the Central Contractor Registration database) and will be asked to provide company certifications and representations in government databases. Keep in mind that in completing these tasks, you aren't making any actual progress towards making a sale. Government buyers don't use databases to find vendors. Instead, the vendors find the buyers.

As much as they would love to ignore it, federal contractors are forced to comply with the government's red tape requirements in order to do business with the government. A recent college graduate or someone in your accounting organization should be able to wade through the red tape. The task may appear daunting at first but, with patience and tenacity, the person assigned the task will come to realize that it's not rocket science. Complying with the government's requirements becomes second nature after the first time through the process.

Your designated person should tackle the following tasks first:

1. Obtain a Dun & Bradstreet Number (DUNS Number) (Go to http://www.dnb.com)

2. Register at the federal Central Contractor Registration web site (Search for Central Contractor Registration in Google)

3. Register at the Online Representations and Certifications Application (ORCA) web site (Search for ORCA - Login in Google)

4. Sign up to receive emails about federal opportunities at the central Federal Business Opportunities site (Search for FedBizOpps in Google)

Do companies need to enlist the services of an attorney when they do business in the federal market? Lawyers have a role to play in the federal market just as they do in the commercial market. The trick is to realize when you need one and when you don't. Don't assume you need one for every little thing you don't understand.

Are special accounting systems required when doing business with the federal government? Yes, you will most likely need one at some point in time but not at the time of market entry. A somewhat generalized accounting package, such as QuikBooks, will do to start. Your business will need to invest in a more specialized accounting system as your involvement in the federal market grows and your revenue increases.

We receive frequent inquiries from companies who tell us they have addressed all of the administrative tasks listed on federal web sites but have failed to receive any federal business. They ask why the orders aren't flowing in from various federal agencies. Our response to such queries is to say be proactive, locate an end user and call them just like you would a commercial customer. Federal buyers are not going to actively seek you out. Decide to make the investment in establishing one-on-one customer relationships or don't waste your money, time, and effort.

Chapter 20

Steps to Take After Winning Your First Federal Contract

Outsider Perception: Although exciting, winning your first federal contract is not really a big deal.

Reality: Winning your first federal contract is critical because it gives your company insider status.

Lesson: Use your coveted insider status, once achieved, to leverage additional sales.

Background:

You won one! You made it through the red tape and hard-fought price negotiations to be awarded a Schedule contract and have made your first sale. Your company is now an insider. Use this position to leverage more sales. Insiders work on-site with their federal customers on a daily basis and can legally look under every stone for more dollars. Use your insider position to nurture your contract into something much, much bigger.

Federal contractors working on-site at a federal facility are in an ideal position to generate more business. Their billable staff sits with the customer every day and, in most cases, gains invaluable intelligence about that customer. On-site personnel also have the opportunity to learn everything there is to know about the customer, the customer's problems, possible fixes, the agency's budget, the agency's procurement plans, and the like. It's all perfectly legal because it is all public information. In this instance, the insider just has much easier access to it.

Perhaps most importantly, a contractor's on-site staff establishes strong relationships with federal customers. Establishing such relationships is critical to success in the federal market and the on-site contractor gets paid to do it. If you were the customer, to whom would you turn if you needed help? You would turn to the people with whom you are working every day, the ones you know and trust.

The federal government doesn't really have a practical way of eliminating the inherent insider edge. It could prohibit the incumbent contractor from re-bidding on existing contracts but this would be disruptive, expensive, and not in the taxpayers' best interests. The moral of the story is to take full advantage of any edge that you have and make it work for you.

Chapter 21

Learn How to Write Federal Proposals

Outsider Perception: Writing a federal proposal is like writing a commercial proposal.

Reality: Federal proposals are a breed unto themselves.

Lesson: Learn to write federal proposals using a business process that integrates proposal writing and sales.

Background:

Learning to prepare outstanding, first-rate proposals is a task that is difficult at best and sometimes bordering on the impossible. Many contractors fail to ever master the assignment. Corporate management must be fully committed to the task and must also devote substantial time and resources to developing and keeping a good writing team. In order to start the process, we recommend doing the following:

1. Sell the opportunity first and then write a proposal. Don't write proposals for projects that you haven't pre-sold.

2. In order to put your best foot forward, present customer-centric proposals based on solutions you have proposed in advance to the federal end user.

3. Make sales and proposal writing an integrated and structured business process. Start the process early and have the proposal started when the actual Request for Proposal (RFP) is published.

4. Propose what the customer wants first; sell them what they need through contract modifications once you've won the contract.

Federal proposal evaluators look for simplicity and reader-friendly proposals; they want just the facts, supported by evidence. Forget the sales fluff. In order to prepare a thorough, well-organized proposal, you must start with an outline. The outline provides the structure needed for your staff to prepare a clear and concise proposal.

As a general rule, proposals are required of service companies but not usually from those offering products. At the onset, a services company will not have to produce that many large or complex proposals because it won't have the experience or organizational capabilities to realistically win the larger opportunities. As the company matures and grows, proposal-writing capabilities become more and more important. Vendors holding pre-approved price list contracts will have to write smaller technical proposals in response to customer requirements. (These proposals will not normally be the larger tomes required to respond to public bids). We recommend taking it slow and learning how to write effective proposals as you grow.

More information on writing federal proposals is included in Appendix D.

Chapter 22

Prosper in the Federal Market

Outsider Perception: The federal market is tough to crack.

Reality: The perception is true.

Lesson: Although the federal market is difficult to tackle, companies that are successful in doing so quickly realize that it's an extremely lucrative one and that their actual sales costs—once they are entrenched—are actually less than in the commercial sector.

Background:

By now you have hopefully concluded that the federal market is not really more difficult to enter than any other new market your business has targeted. Don't let the fear of the unknown hold you back. Market entry requires tenacity and patience. The federal market offers rewards commensurate with the effort your staff puts into delving into this new endeavor. For highly-focused companies, the rewards can be exceptionally rich and lucrative.

Keep in mind that federal buyers will never get rid of companies that perform at the highest levels because trusted performers make the buyers' professional lives easier and risk free. Happy buyers will go out of their way to make sure that your company remains their business partner. The partnership truly begins when your company wins its first contract and, once this occurs, your company has total control over its destiny in the market. It is entirely possible for a small business working in the federal market to grow to become a $100 million business in just a few years.

Small business preference programs can dramatically impact your company's growth. Companies that cannot take advantage of preference programs take heart—companies without the benefit of preferences have also experienced explosive growth.

The critical steps to success in the federal market are:

1. Sell to federal customers as you would in the commercial market.

2. Learn the rules for closing federal sales.

3. Get a GSA Schedule contract and sell with a pre-approved price list.

4. Target federal customers in your region first and become an "insider" like the large federal prime contractors.

5. Use the inherent advantages of being an insider to help your business succeed in the federal market.

6. Certify your company as a preferred small business if it qualifies.

Most federal experts predict that the small business market may reach $100 billion or more soon. There are also rumblings in Congress about helping small businesses more than in the past. The women-owned small business preference program may finally be implemented once the current administration leaves office. Congress is working on other legislative changes that will put more teeth in rules that require large businesses to subcontract with small businesses, and something might actually be done about the large businesses that mask themselves as small. If pressed to make a prediction, I would say that the next five years are going to be even better for small businesses than during the Bush administration.

Appendix A

Finding Federal End Users Who Buy What You Sell

Knowing your customers is the key to sales success. This is true whether you're selling to public or private organizations. The most successful federal contractors take the time to uncover contact information for the buyers who purchase what their company sells. However, finding the right buyers can be one of the most difficult aspects of federal sales and is the single biggest reason that small businesses find the federal market so difficult to enter.

The federal government offers a wide range of marginally-useful resources to help small businesses enter the federal market. For example, federal agency web sites provide information on how to do business with the government. The reality is that these web sites, for the most part, provide nothing more than suggestions on how to deal with red tape. Federal agencies also hold conferences and training events for small businesses. Unfortunately, end user contact information is not provided as part of these events. The government's offerings are carefully designed to provide help on the surface without providing access to end users. Why, you ask? The truth is that end users would prefer to remain anonymous because they have all the vendors they need and do not want to be deluged with calls from new vendors.

A long-range solution to this problem may be in the making. Congress is currently considering legislation which would require the creation and posting of a public contract awards database. The proposed database would provide a summary of what was purchased and who the end users and official buyers were for awarded contracts. The creation of the proposed database would be the single biggest step the federal government has ever taken to truly opening the federal market. However, the implementation of such a database could take several years, if not more.

In the interim, a small business is forced to conduct research by (i) searching the Internet, (ii) perusing agency telephone directories and agency organizational charts, and (iii) making contact with contracting officers to ask them who the federal buyers are in their respective agencies. Fedmarket.com provides an alternative to the methods described above, FedBuying Intelligence. We offer a contract award database that identifies the contracting offices that buy what small businesses sell. FedBuying Intelligence searches five years of public bid data and tells you who bought what. Official buyer contact data, including the buyer's telephone number and email address, is provided in a spreadsheet that can be downloaded.

Procedures for Finding End Users

Contact data for end users— the people making the purchasing decisions for complex products and solutions—is not readily available to the public. Once located, matters are further complicated by the fact that there can be more than one federal official responsible for making purchasing decisions for a large buy. Contracting officers and their colleagues, known as contracting specialists, can be identified by the products or services they have purchased in the past. With respect to identifying potential customers, use the contracting officer as the official point of contact between you and the government. Although they know who the end users are, these officials may be reluctant to divulge the information to you. A typical conversation with a contracting officer might go like this:

Vendor: "I see from my research that you awarded a $500,000 contract on May 11, 2005 to Acme Reseller, Inc. The product purchased under that contract was Cisco routers. Who was the end user in your office?"

Contracting officer: "I don't really know and I would have to dig out the contract to find out."

Vendor: "I would appreciate it if you would do that and call me back."

Contracting officer: "I'll try but I can't promise you anything due to our office's overwhelming workload."

Vendor: "But I thought that the contracting officer is the single point of contact for vendors and that your job is to promote competition."

Contracting officer: "You are correct on both counts but that doesn't mean that I can answer end user questions for the thousands of vendors out there."

Based on the tenor of the discussions above, it is unlikely that the contracting officer will actually get back to the vendor with the information requested. The issue of whether the contracting officer is legally required to give out an end user's name is gray. The public has the legal right to request a copy of the contract itself under the Freedom of Information Act (FOIA). However, expect to wait from one to twelve months for a response. By the time you get a copy of the contract, the end user will have ordered another large batch of Cisco routers. Although FOIA mandates that federal officials respond to FOIA requests within 20 business days, this rule is routinely ignored. The bottom line is the feds have all the cards so you have to find a way to play their game. Trying to force them to give you contact data is counterproductive.

Appendix B

The People in the Federal Sales Process and Their Motivations

Buyers in the commercial and federal sectors behave in the same manner. Most buyers will choose the path of least resistance and then run to get to their kids' soccer games on time. Federal buyers view obtaining the best value for the taxpayer as a noble objective but hold maximizing their own raises and performance evaluations on an even higher plane.

Experienced federal sales people know that the roles people play and their motivations profoundly affect buying decisions. Most people are motivated by self-interest; that's not necessarily a good or bad thing, it's just a fact. The desire to do a good job, to avoid failure, and to save money on behalf of the taxpayer benefits us all. Having a clear picture of the various roles of the people in the federal sales game may help you better target your sales approach.

Person	Responsibilities	Primary Motivation	Not Motivated To:
Federal end user	Performing a job for the taxpayer in the most efficient, cost-effective manner possible	Successfully accomplishing work tasks and being rewarded with raises and promotions	Select an unknown vendor or one who represents a potential risk
	Monitoring contractor performance	Avoiding risk, ensuring that buying decisions produce the desired outcome	
Contracting officer	Legal responsibility for a contract (signs contract)	Successfully accomplishing work tasks and being	Contract with a vendor which was selected in violation

Person	Responsibilities	Primary Motivation	Not Motivated To:
	Ensuring that requirements for competitive bids have been met Monitoring contract performance	rewarded with raises and promotions Ensuring that all rules and regulations have been followed Maintaining a contract file that shows maximum possible competition took place	of the rules
Small business specialist (advocate)	Advocating the use of small businesses	Promoting the use of small businesses as a policy	Help a particular small business win a contract
Members of Congress and the White House	Develop and pass legislation Represent constituents Contract performance	Re-election Votes and campaign dollars Bring major projects into their own states or districts More contract dollars Controlling the customer relationship	Help a particular small business win a contract unless the exercise is directly connected to more votes or money Subcontract with companies that do not bring contract dollars or that threaten the customer relationship

How Purchasing Decisions Are Made

Like all of us, the people who make buying decisions in the federal government are influenced by their own biases, perceptions, and views of the world. Although the government uses an ostensibly objective numeric scoring system to evaluate proposals, in the end it's a person who assigns the score. The process is not that different from when your teachers graded you back in grade school. A proposal evaluator reads a submitted resume and decides the person on the resume is graded given a score of 87 out of 100. Why not an 85 or 89? Because it is a subjective process and all procurement decisions boil down to a subjective judgment no matter how sophisticated the scoring scheme. Scoring usually doesn't occur when products are purchased, but essentially the same thing happens.

A buyer may say that product pricing, a particular feature, a fast delivery time, or the availability of an extended warranty is his basis for selecting Product A over Product B. In fact, Product A and B may be virtually identical; the difference is that the seller of Product A employed a more effective sales approach. Whether buying one million paperclips or a $10 million software system, the most important factor in making the sale is usually what the buyer has learned from salespeople.

A salesperson's goal is to make a sale by helping buyers make informed decisions. Information garnered from a vendor's references, from colleagues who have past experience with a vendor, and the general reputation and brand identity of the vendor all contribute to what comes down to a buyer's subjective decision based on value.

Appendix C

GSA Schedules – A Vendor's Path to Federal Sales

The GSA Schedules program, also known as the Federal Supply Schedule program, was initiated by the federal government in an effort to simplify the process of acquiring needed goods and services. The program has been highly successful to the point that it is now the favored purchasing mechanism used by government buyers. A federal buyer who elects to use the more traditional procurement method of putting an opportunity out for public bid has to wait upwards of one year before an actual contract is executed. In contrast, a Schedule purchase can be effectuated in a matter of days or a couple of weeks.

A Schedule contract is a five-year contract containing three, five-year renewal options. In total, if the government were to exercise all three options, the term of the contract would span twenty years. Although a Schedule contract is an official federal contract, it is not funded until such time as purchase orders are placed through the contract. As such, the onus is on the Schedule contract holder to actively solicit orders from federal buyers. Schedule contractors that do not meet GSA's stated $25,000.00 minimum in annual Schedule sales run the risk of having their contract terminated. The Schedule program is funded by GSA's assessment of a 0.75% fee, or "Industrial Funding Fee," on each dollar sold under a vendor's GSA Schedule contract. Vendors must report their Schedule sales to GSA on a quarterly basis and must also pay the appropriate Industrial Funding Fee at the same time.

At present, there are approximately 55 different general categories of products or services that may be sold to the government under the Schedule program. This list includes office products, information technology equipment, building supplies, medical equipment, chemical supplies, and a host of professional services (such as legal, management consulting, accounting, and professional engineering services). Certain industries, such as architectural design or construction services, are not covered by the Schedule program.

In order to become a Schedule supplier, a vendor must go through an arduous application process. The most difficult and painstaking part of the Schedule application and approval process is negotiating what the government and vendor agree is a "fair and reasonable price" for the vendor's offered products or services. For this reason, some vendors choose to hire consultants to assist them in the preparation and negotiation of the contract. Many report back that the expense for such consultants was money well spent as the entire submission and approval process can be extremely costly in terms of time and employee stress levels.

Once a particular Schedule contract is awarded, the successful vendor is placed on a list of approved suppliers for that particular Schedule. Federal agency buyers can then order from a vendor using GSA Advantage!, the government's online "shopping mall" for GSA Schedule products and services. A common misconception is that only GSA employees can make a purchase through a Schedule contract. This is not true; virtually any federal buyer can buy from GSA Schedule holders. Congress has also granted state and local agencies the authority to purchase through the Information Technology Schedule contract (known as the "IT 70 Schedule"). State and local purchasing authority may be extended to other GSA Schedules in the future.

Making a purchase through a Schedule contract is relatively easy. A federal buyer interested in a particular Schedule holder's products or services sends a Request for Quote to the company's designated GSA contract point person. In response, the company prepares a quote using its approved GSA Schedule contract prices as its pricing basis. The buyer, upon making a final decision as to which vendor he wishes to use, then places a purchase order against the vendor's GSA Schedule contract. The purchase order is then sent directly to the vendor.

Unlike a public procurement, competition in the GSA Schedule arena is significantly less because (i) a buyer need only procure three quotes from GSA Schedule holders prior to making a purchase, and (ii) the three prospective vendors' contract pricing is pre-determined. For this reason, many vendors believe that purchase orders will begin to roll in immediately after contract award and without the necessity of any further action on their part. This expectation is unrealistic. Schedule contract holders must actively sell their company's capabilities to prospective federal buyers. Schedule vendors should not expect to have sales under their Schedule contracts without focused, agency-based sales efforts.

Why Federal Buyers Like GSA Schedules

Because purchasing from a Schedule vendor is quick and efficient, sales under the Schedule program are skyrocketing. GSA's Information Technology Division, the most successful division in the program, reports that fiscal year 2004 sales for their division alone totaled approximately $17 billion. Federal buyers report that pre-negotiated pricing is one of the key factors to the success of the program. Furthermore, buyers rave about the efficiency of the process and the significant reduction in paperwork and red tape associated with Schedule buys. Lastly, Schedule purchases are transacted behind the scenes without much scrutiny from non-participating vendors. This "secrecy" cuts down on costly vendor protests.

Why Vendors Like GSA Schedules

GSA Schedule contracts are an ideal contracting vehicle for small businesses that cannot afford to obtain more than one multiple award Schedule contract. Vendors like Schedule contracts for the same reasons that federal buyers do: The Schedule program reduces competition, allows vendors to avoid public bids (thereby saving vast sums in proposal development costs), and allows contractors to close a deal within weeks instead of waiting months on end for an award of a public bid.

Drawbacks

GSA Schedule contracts do have drawbacks. Obtaining one can cost in excess of $15,000. The return on this investment is low unless a company has substantial annual Schedule contract sales. Other drawbacks include:

- A Schedule contract reduces a vendor's commercial pricing flexibility and may result in reduced profits.

- Your ability to increase your GSA contract prices is restricted by the terms of the contract.

- The terms of the Schedule contract require that the vendor carefully monitor and control its commercial discounting practices. Indiscriminate or random/spot commercial discounting can lead to automatic reductions in GSA contract prices.

- A GSA Schedule contract may be terminated if a business does not meet the annual sales threshold of $25,000.00.

- Schedule orders must be carefully tracked and accounted for to ensure that the proper Industrial Funding Fee is paid at the end of each quarter.

Drawbacks aside, a GSA Schedule is the selling vehicle of choice for small businesses. An aggressive company willing to devote dollar and manpower resources to developing federal business can reap great rewards through its GSA Schedule contract.

Appendix D

More on Proposal Writing

Why is Proposal Writing So Difficult?

Many people don't like to write; this can become particularly apparent when it comes to writing complex federal proposals. Those given proposal writing assignments tend to postpone their writing tasks; in the case of your technical people, writing may be something they've avoided with a passion their entire lives.

Federal proposal writing can be a very costly process. To do it well, a company must have a Proposal Manager with extensive experience and good writing and management skills. It certainly helps if your Proposal Manager has patience, is persistent, and possesses a calm demeanor under pressure. Such traits are difficult to find in one person. Unfortunately, the Proposal Manager usually can't write the subject matter solution (called the "Technical Approach") required by the customer. The drafting of the Technical Approach requires the participation of technical specialists and, unfortunately, many lack good writing skills because their educational focus was targeted elsewhere.

Proposal Writing Mistakes

The process of producing a quality proposal is inherently prone to problems. It's difficult to manage the process, and costly. When a company does not win a bid opportunity, staff morale often suffers.

Mistakes made by most companies include:

- Inadequate funding and an insufficient dedication of staffing resources to the project

- Management's failure to provide adequate leadership and moral support

- Deciding to write proposals that never had a chance of winning because the company did not have a pre-existing relationship with the customer

- Not having a highly structured, integrated sales and writing process

- A lack of understanding of "defensive" proposal writing

- The absence of an experienced Proposal Manager

- Not having an incentive system and structure in place that motivates your technical staff to write effectively

The sections that follow discuss how you must change your corporate thinking to change the way proposals are written within your company.

Why Proposals Exist

Why do proposals even exist? Contrary to popular belief, proposals are not written so federal evaluators can select the best, high-value solution to their problem. Instead, proposals are prepared by contractors and submitted because the Federal Acquisition Regulations (FAR) require that this procedure be followed in order to document that a competition was held.

Why aren't proposals used as a method to find the best solution? The answer lies in the fact that, for services solicitations at least, the decision on the eventual contract winner has often been made far in advance of the time the proposals are written. The agency wants an incumbent contractor back to eliminate any disruption in operations. Nonetheless, the agency is required by regulation to hold a public competition. Although the end user knows and trusts its existing solution provider, the contracting officer may demand that a public competition take place. In this situation, the winning company has to write a defensive proposal to defend their pre-established position with the customer. Does the contracting officer care about the number of trees that went into the losing proposals? Not really.

The eventual winner of the contract is not always predetermined. However, don't lie awake at night counting the revenue that you are going to receive from blind bids. You may win a small percentage, but you will spend way too much money writing losing proposals and, equally importantly, burn out your staff in the process. Is there a better solution?

Multiple award Schedule contracts like GSA's Schedule program are a partial solution, but don't look for any revolutionary solutions anytime soon. The political pressure to keep up an appearance of competition is too intense.

Why a Federal Proposal is Different

Federal Requests for Proposals (RFPs) are unique because they are:

- Long, lengthy, and full of boilerplate and clauses

- Not written clearly

- Not well organized

- Full of detailed, yet confusing, requirements

Federal RFPs are evaluated by a formal evaluation committee using a point scoring scheme. Although numeric, the point scoring scheme requires a subjective judgment on the part of an evaluator and is subject to the evaluator's personal views, experience, and biases. Most importantly, it is highly likely that the evaluators have met with vendors and have knowledge of each vendor's suggested solutions to their problem.

These conditions make writing a federal proposal a unique process. A federal proposal must (i) be written with the customer in mind, (ii) meet each and every requirement outlined in the RFP, and (iii) provide only what the RFP asks for. In short, it must be responsive, compelling, and defensive (as in, designed not to lose).

Responding to a federal RFP is like renovating a home. It is a complex task and typically requires double or triple the effort originally estimated. There are no magic bullets. Writing a responsive, winning proposal requires a structured, systematic approach. Large prime contractors have developed their own approaches to proposal development. Smaller companies gradually piece together an approach but their proposal efforts usually are somewhat random. The market for proposal-writing software is saturated with "convince them that you are the best" templates. The templates are designed for commercial proposals and are ineffective for federal proposals.

Write Defensive Proposals

Most authorities on writing federal proposals define a defensive proposal as follows:

- One written with the goal of being the last proposal standing

- An offering that presents a practical solution from the customer's perspective

- One that gives the customer what they want; no more and no less

- A bid that addresses each and every requirement of the RFP

- A proposal that is clear, concise, and devoid of sales puffery

Another definition of a defensive proposal is one that defends the position that you have already taken with the customer. Ideally, you have met with the customer, identified their requirements, and proposed a solution that meets their requirements. When your company writes the proposal, it must prove that your business can do what your sales people told the customer it could do during the sales process. In other words, you close the deal with words and provable facts and assure the customer that they will minimize their risk by choosing your company. You may have sold one or more of the people on the evaluation committee. Now you need to sell the rest.

Don't bid if you haven't established a position to defend. You can count on the fact that one or more vendors have established positions. Attendees at our seminars lament that they can't get to the customer because there are too many prime contractors and other competitors trying to do the same thing. Welcome to the world of direct sales and hard knocks. Either power your way through the flack, or don't play in the market.

Process Versus Content

Proposal writing involves both process and content. Effective writing processes are important but proposal content rules over process. Your company can develop a proposal smoothly and on time, with minimal hassle and without last-minute crises, and submit a product that is beautifully formatted with fancy graphics. Yet you could still lose due to lack of "responsive content."

A responsive proposal contains all of the content and information that was asked for in the RFP. The content must be presented in a concise manner and should demonstrate how your proposed solution is going to solve the customer's problem or otherwise address his or her needs. This, of course, begs the question of how a business discerns what the customer wants. The answer to this query is that you can only do so through aggressive sales and by using the customer intelligence gathered during the sales process.

Defensive proposals present an easily understood and direct solution that addresses the requirements of the RFP. The information is presented in a clear and concise manner substantiated with provable facts presented without embellishment.

Many of the attendees at Fedmarket's seminars were federal proposal evaluators while employed by the government. Without exception, they say that a federal proposal should not attempt to "gild the lily"—in other words, proposals should not contain:

- Unsubstantiated sales pitches

- Fancy bindings, graphics, and tab systems

- Information that was not requested in the RFP

Evaluators are intelligent, hard-working people who want you to make their job easy. Extraneous information and frill will not have the intended impact. In fact, it actually works against you because it makes the evaluator work harder to discern your message. Graphics can be used but only if they make the presentation clearer and more concise. Do not add graphics merely in an attempt to impress the reader.

Evaluators tell us that if they ask for two resumes, they literally want your company to submit two resumes. When they ask for three past experience descriptions, provide three. Resist the temptation to provide six under the assumption that more is better. Providing additional project descriptions is more likely to annoy the evaluators than make your company appear infinitely more experienced and capable than your competitors.

Providing a compelling Technical Approach is the key to a winning proposal. You can create a good Technical Approach using traditional outlining techniques and story boards, and by developing winning themes and subthemes. To do this, it is imperative that the Proposal Manager develops an overall proposal outline, and then pulls together and edits the disparate technical material developed by a number of technical specialists. The three O's of writing effective federal proposals are Outlining, Outlining, and Outlining.